The World of Work

Choosing a Career in Music

Many people dream of a career in the field of music. It takes a lot of time and energy to make the dream come true.

The World of Work
Choosing a Career in Music

John Giacobello

THE ROSEN PUBLISHING GROUP, INC.
NEW YORK

Published in 1997, 1999 by The Rosen Publishing Group, Inc.
29 East 21st Street, New York, NY 10010

Revised Edition 1999

Library of Congress Cataloging-in-Publication Data

Giacobello, John.
    Choosing a Career in music / John Giacobello.
       p.   cm.—(The world of work)
    Includes bibliographical references and index.
    Summary: Offers an overview of careers in the field of music, from singing to songwriting to recording.
    ISBN 0-8239-3000-9
    1. Music—Vocational guidance—Juvenile literature. [1. Music—Vocational guidance. 2. Vocational guidance.] I. Title. II. Series: World of work (New York, N.Y.)
    ML3790.G515 1996
    780'.23'73—dc20   96-17496
                                                          CIP
                                                      AC MN

Manufactured in the United States of America

Contents

Introduction

Many people believe that pursuing a career in the music industry is impractical, irresponsible, and nearly impossible. But they may be familiar only with certain aspects of some music careers: financial ups and downs, a constant struggle to find work, the hectic life of a rock star that only a few fortunate souls actually achieve. There are actually many sides to the diverse field of music, sides that are worth exploring even for those without musical talent or ambitions for stardom.

For example, for the business-minded music lover there are opportunities in talent scouting, publicity, retail sales, and more. Many of these jobs can offer a high degree of security not normally associated with the music field, yet one can be surrounded by the energy and excitement of music throughout the nine-to-five workday.

Those with technical expertise might consider music recording, engineering, or producing. These can be fulfilling ways to contribute to the sound of a recorded piece of music or a live performance. These days, many producers are considered great artists in their own right.

Writers can try their hand at music journalism and report the hottest scoops on musicians of all kinds. Skilled and patient musicians can work as music teachers. Disc jockeys and video jockeys spin tunes and visuals, music publishers buy and sell songs, managers help to guide the careers of musicians…and this is only a small sampling of career possibilities.

And of course creating music, while definitely not an easy road, can be a satisfying and lucrative career for the right person.

If you approach the careers outlined in this book with an open mind, you may just be surprised to find many open doors for responsible, practical individuals like you. Music is a world where anything is possible.

Questions to Ask Yourself

Choosing a career is one challenge of the high school years. 1) Have you made your choice yet? 2) Have you explored several areas of interest? 3) Are you considering music?

Many people continue their study of music in college or in private lessons.

Making Music

Although there are many kinds of career opportunities in the *music industry*, let's begin with the one most people think of first: making music. This is the creation of the product. It is the reason the entire industry came about.

If this is where your talents and dreams lie, this chapter will give you an idea of what to do, how to do it, and what to expect. Most musicians will probably agree that it is a difficult way to make a living. But talent and creativity are always in high demand.

Making Popular Music

Who doesn't want to be a star? Glamour, excitement, fame, and fortune draw many young people to the stage each year. Many hope that they will become *recording artists*.

And although many would disagree, this really is a career choice. It is also one of the most difficult career choices. Hard work, determination, and talent may propel you to the top of the charts. Then again, they may not.

What determines whether or not you make it as a recording artist is often luck. Simply being at the right place at the right time is what allowed many of today's music stars to be where they are now. For example, pop legend Madonna left for New York City with little money and few friends. She met a disc jockey, or DJ. He played her demonstration tape at a popular dance club. It caught on. She was signed by a record company shortly thereafter.

Stardom Doesn't Come Easy

You may decide that becoming a recording artist is your dream. If so, and if you are determined to make it happen, count on that determination. You will probably need it to see you through years of struggling. Becoming a recording artist usually takes time. Chances are you will need a day job, at least at first. For this reason, make sure you develop your nonmusical skills as well.

After you graduate, a job in a restaurant or retail store will allow you to pay your rent and bills. This should leave you enough extra time to practice and perform, both of which you

Superstars, such as Madonna, had to work hard for many years to become as successful as they are.

should do as often as possible. You might play at clubs, parties, or festivals. You might also play for hospitals or charity functions.

It is important to have a demonstration tape, or *demo*, of your music. This is what you will usually play for club owners and event organizers. You can pay a *recording studio* to help you create your demo. Or you can buy your own inexpensive multi-track recorder and make one yourself.

The next step is to get the attention of a record company to sign with. Record companies have *talent scouts*. They are known as A&R representatives. They look for new performers. That is why performing live is essential. You can also mail or hand-deliver your demo to record companies. Chapter 5 discusses this process in greater detail.

It is difficult to estimate a salary range for a recording artist. When you start out, you will probably have to perform for free. After that, you could make anywhere from $50 to $5,000 or more for each show. If you are signed by a record company and become successful, the sky is the limit. Music lessons are not required but they can help.

Whether they specialize in world music, rap, or heavy metal, record companies work basically the same way. And they are all looking for talented artists.

Performing on the Side

If stardom is not your goal but you do love to perform, you may want to consider another idea: keep your day job and join a group for weekend engagements. There are opportunities for bands at school dances, in nightclubs, on cruise ships, at weddings or bar mitzvahs, and at countless other engagements. It can be an excellent source of extra income and fun.

I Write the Songs

You don't have to be a musician or a singer to feel the thrill of hearing one of your songs played on the radio or on TV! Some people just write songs for other artists to perform. They are known as *songwriters.*

Debra, Song Writer

When I was in high school I really loved to write poetry. Words and ideas just came to me. I enjoyed rearranging them until they expressed something I was feeling or imagining. Once I wrote a poem that had a lot of rhythm. I imagined what it would sound like set to music.

It was good, so I thought, "Hey! I might be on to something." I wanted to make sure nobody could steal my song. My dad said to send it to myself via certified registered mail. When I received it, I never opened it—the postmark is like a copyright, which proves that I wrote the song. Ask your post office how to do this.

I have some friends who are musicians. They got together and recorded the song for me. It sounded great! Then I played my demo for other local bands. I also checked the library for addresses of record companies all over the country. Then I sent them the tape with my name, address, and phone number.

Nothing happened for a long time. Then an A&R woman from an independent record company called. She offered to buy the rights to the song. An independent record company is a small company, not one of the major ones. The song never became a hit, but it did make it onto an album. So I'm going to keep writing as much as I can in my spare time. Maybe someday I can make it as a full-time songwriter.

It isn't easy to become successful as a songwriter, so you should always have something to fall back on. The pay varies, depending on how many of your songs are bought and how popular they become.

Making Classical Music

It is fairly difficult to land a position in an orchestra. The competition is tough, and you need to be a top-notch musician. Even then job prospects are few. The best way to start out is as a *section member*. Once you are in the orchestra, you will learn how to advance to *section leader* or *conductor*.

Playing an instrument in your school orchestra is a good way to get experience performing classical music.

Sylvester, Flute Player

I started playing the flute when I was twelve years old. I practiced all the time and became very good at reading music and learning songs. Now, at twenty, I am a section member in an orchestra. Several other players and I make up the flute section of the orchestra. I need to memorize my parts of the performances before we even practice.

I follow the conductor's cues. The conductor is the most important person in the orchestra, because he prepares us all for our performances. He leads us during the show using his arms and body movements.

I also need to pay attention to my section leader. She decides things like what parts certain section members should play and how we should play them. I really enjoy being a part of the orchestra making beautiful music.

You can look for auditions in *International Musician*, the journal of the American Federation of Musicians. This journal also lists scholarships, fellowships, competitions, and seminars. *Symphony Magazine* is another excellent resource.

According to the American Symphony Orchestra League, more than 1,800 symphony orchestras in the United States employ musicians. Most regional orchestras pay between $400 and $700 per week, while major ones may pay members $1,000 to $1,200 and up weekly. Salaries are generally higher for conductors, the most successful of whom make as much as $500,000 per year.

There are other opportunities for classically trained musicians. Like rock and dance groups, other types of musicians may play weekend engagements for extra money. Weddings, bar mitzvahs, and ballrooms are just a few examples of places where you can pick up extra cash for playing all types of music.

Making Religious Music

Most religions include some type of music as part of their services. You may wish to provide that music as a part- or full-time career. Becoming this sort of musician can be fulfilling, especially if you are religious.

If you work as a *church organist*, you can make anywhere from $15,000 to $50,000 per year, depending on the size of the congregation and how often you play. Weddings and funerals usually pay between $50 and $100 per service. No college education is required, although organ or piano training is helpful. Talk to the music directors at any religious organizations you are interested in working with.

A singer with a college degree and a good knowledge of Hebrew and the Jewish faith has an excellent chance of becoming the *cantor* of a temple or synagogue. The cantor leads all the prayers in Jewish ceremonies, and those prayers are generally sung. Salaries for successful cantors are very good, ranging from $24,000 to $70,000. If you are interested, you may be able to receive financial aid for training to become a cantor through a synagogue or temple. Speak to other cantors in your area about getting started.

Norman, Choir Director

I used to go to church every Sunday. I really enjoyed the choir music, so I started practicing hymns at home. I met the choir members, and they persuaded me to join. So I sang with them regularly and paid close attention to the choir director. She's the person who organized the choir for our weekly and holiday performances. When she moved away, the rest of the choir members agreed that I should be the one to take her place.

The job pays well, and I love helping the singers to sound their best. It does take up a lot of my time, so I'm glad I enjoy it. Most of my weekends are spent rehearsing.

A *choir director* can make anywhere from $15,000 to $65,000 per year. The best way to get involved is by speaking with the choir directors at your local churches and starting out as a choir member.

Some Lesser Known Careers

Have you ever heard of an arranger, an orchestrator, or a copyist? These are some musical careers that few people know about. But for the right person, any one of them could be just the right opportunity.

Teens who enjoy singing can gain experience by singing in a school chorus or church choir.

An *arranger* is a person who knows a lot about reading and writing music. The job is to take a song that has already been written and to arrange its parts. What instrument plays which part, and how is it played? How fast should the song be? What kind of rhythm should be used? These are all questions the arranger must answer.

As an arranger you would probably work free-lance, which means that you may be hired by recording artists, performers, or music publishers. You could also arrange music for movies or television. Pay starts low, about

$11,000 to $15,000 per year. Of course, the money increases as you get more work and become better known.

The only education required is an understanding of music theory. You can learn it through college courses or classes at a local music school. The best way to get started is by writing your own music, then arranging it. Offer to arrange for local groups, or perhaps a musical play in your area.

An arranger sometimes also works as an *orchestrator.* This is a person who transposes music. Transposing means changing the music written for one group, orchestra, or vocalist so that it suits another performer. Orchestrating requires that you know music theory.

After the arranger arranges and the orchestrator transposes, the music needs to be copied onto a staff. A staff is the five-line pattern on which the notes are drawn in a musical composition. This is the job of the *copyist.* A copyist must be able to write out a composition neatly, without making any mistakes.

Orchestrators' and copyists' salaries depend on how much work they do. For job openings, check the classified sections in music magazines or newspapers. Posting flyers in music stores can also be helpful. The key is making that first

A person who is first learning how to play an instrument plays music that is arranged simply.

contact. After that, the more you work, the more successful you could become.

Music Education

If you decide to seek musical training, you may be wondering where to turn. The most inexpensive teachers can usually be hired through music stores or ads in the classified section of your local newspaper.

If you can go to college, an applied music or music education program will give you a broad range of music classes. *Applied music* focuses on performance, composition, and theory. *Music education* teaches you how to teach music. You can enroll in these and other programs through colleges or *conservatories*. Conservatories generally provide a higher quality of music education.

Questions to Ask Yourself

Music offers many kinds of careers. 1) Do you think you would be happiest playing an instrument? If so, in a band? In an orchestra? 2) Do ideas for songs come to your mind? 3) If you are active in your religion, would you like to sing in the chorus or play the organ or become a cantor?

Recording Music

2

The next time you pop in your favorite CD or cassette, think about the work that must have gone into creating it. As you dance to the pounding drums and slick bass notes, imagine what it would be like to help put those sounds together. There are many ways for you to be involved in musical recording. And there are several career opportunities available.

Backing Up Others

If you are skilled at reading music and can learn songs quickly, you might be able to become a *studio musician*, or *session musician*. The job involves backing up other bands and performers that are making studio recordings. You must play exactly what they show you, exactly the way they tell you to play it. In addition, sometimes you might perform with the bands on stage, or work on television or radio commercials.

Recording engineers make sure that the music recorded in a studio sounds the way the performer wants it to.

These same opportunities also exist for *backup singers.* It is helpful to be able to sing many different styles of music so you can increase your chances of getting work.

For both of these positions, salaries depend on how much you work and how popular you become. When you start out, you may have to work for free. Studio musicians and backup singers who are established make around $100 per hour, and sessions usually last around three hours.

These jobs are rewarding for many people because they make a living doing something they enjoy. However, this type of artist has no opportunity to use her or his own creativity. This can be frustrating.

This may be something you think you could accept and enjoy. If so, the best way to get started is to put an ad in a newspaper. A music-oriented one would be best. Or apply for a job in a recording studio to answer phones or assist the manager. This will help you to get your foot in the door.

Engineering Recorded Music

You may love and want to work in the music industry. But you may not be a musician. You may be good with machinery, and may enjoy figuring out the way things work. You may pick up on technical language very quickly.

Even though you don't play an instrument, you know how music should sound. A job engineering music in a recording studio may be for you.

Step One: Assistant Engineer

A good way to get started in a recording studio is as an *assistant engineer*. In this position you get the studio ready for the musicians coming in to record. This includes plugging in the right number of mikes, instruments, amps, monitors, and anything else

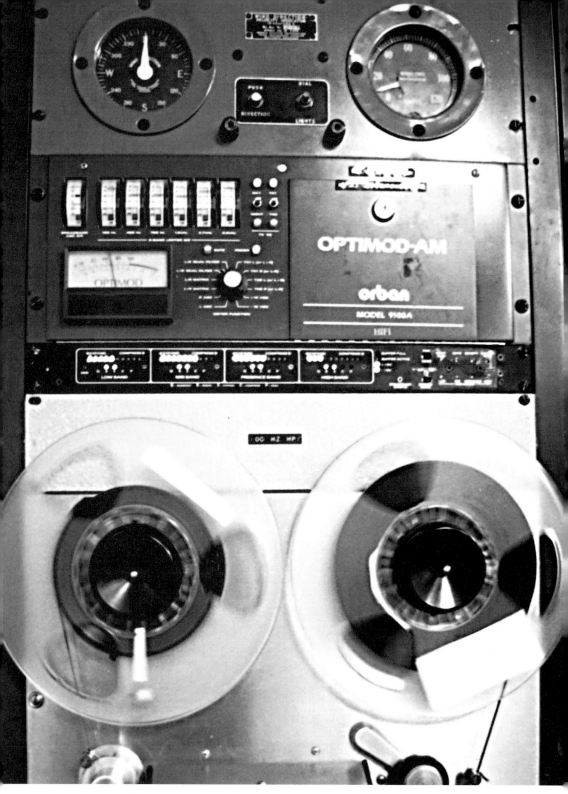

An assistant engineer makes sure all the equipment in a recording studio is ready for the musicians and the recording engineer to use.

being used in the recording. It may involve heavy lifting.

The engineer may also give you other tasks, such as assisting during the actual recording. This is a good way to learn how recordings are made. The salary is around $12,000 or less. If you are promoted to the position of recording engineer, the pay should increase.

Movin' on Up: Engineer

The *recording engineer* operates the recording equipment in the studio. It is his or her job to make the recording sound the way the performer wants it to sound. The best way to learn how to do this is by example. Pay very close attention when you are the engineer's assistant or apprentice.

After the recording has been made, the engineer must mix the tracks (each instrument's part) so that the recording sounds balanced.

Most engineers make from $15,000 to $35,000 per year. Exceptional engineers with experience and good reputations in the industry can make $50,000 or more. The highest-paid engineers (working with the biggest stars) earn more than $100,000.

The Top of the Ladder: Producer

The next move up is to *record producer.* The

producer oversees the entire recording process. In this position, you would have several responsibilities. First you work with the artist(s) to choose the right songs to record. Then you must choose a studio and make an appointment. The producer hires other people to assist in the recording—musicians, backup singers, and engineers.

Rowell, Record Producer

After fifteen years of working in recording studios, I finally made it as a free-lance record producer. This means that I am hired by record companies and artists to produce their records.

I work closely with engineers to help shape the sounds of the bands we produce. I also take care of the business end of the recording process, which includes making sure the recording stays under its budget and all material is copyrighted.

Record producers earn a fee of $5,000 to $40,000 per album and up, plus a royalty of 2 percent to 4 percent on the record's sales. The salary can be much higher for top-notch producers working with the biggest stars. You will need some recording studio experience. Learn how to produce songs by watching others, and find your way around the studio equipment while doing other jobs. Then stay on the lookout for opportunity!

Questions to Ask Yourself

Making music takes more than the musician. 1) Would you like to be a studio musician and back up performers? 2) Are you mechanically inclined and interested in how music is recorded? 3) Would you like to learn enough about the business to become a producer?

Selling Music

3

Sometimes Tina feels there are two people inside of her. One wants to work in an office and have a job that challenges her problem-solving skills. The other person wants to be surrounded by the excitement and energy of music all the time. She wishes she could bring those two people together.

An excellent career opportunity may be waiting for Tina in the music industry. Many business-oriented positions are available in music. They could offer the best of both worlds to the right person.

Those Magical Letters: A&R

In chapter 1, we explained how important it is to be seen and heard by an *A&R person* at a record company. What does A&R mean? Well, the initials stand for Artist and Repertoire, but that doesn't tell you very much.

An A&R person is basically a talent scout.

Many musicians perform as much as possible in hopes that an A&R person, or talent scout, will discover them.

His job is to find new artists for the record company to sign. *Signing an artist* means that the artist signs a contract in which he or she promises to sell records through that company only. In return, the company helps the artist promote and sell the music.

A&R representatives may also search for new songs. These representatives listen to demo tapes that are sent to them. They attend performances at bars and nightclubs. Sometimes they try to sign artists who are already with other record companies by making them a better offer.

This job requires a natural ability to spot

An A&R company promotes their recording artists by getting disc jockeys to play their artists' songs on the air.

potential hit songs and successful acts. It is also important to work well with other people and to have at least a high school diploma. It is not an easy job to find. Pay may start low, around $18,000, but the rewards for hard work can be great. Top A&R representatives make up to $90,000, and sometimes more.

To get started in A&R, it is important to read as much as you can. Stay current on all trends in the industry. What was more popular among young audiences in 1997, R&B or alternative rock? What about this year? Will electronica stay in the mainstream? Is glam-rock making a comeback?

These are the types of questions you should be able to answer, or at least have your own ideas about. And your ideas will be stronger if you are well informed.

Also, check with record companies for internships and other types of jobs, such as messenger or receptionist. This is a good approach, since most of these companies promote from within.

From Discovery to Promotion

Once new talent is discovered, the artists need for their songs to be heard by as many new ears as possible. This is where the record company's *promotion person,* or *promotion staffer,* comes in. This person works to get the company's new records played on the radio. It is very similar to a sales job. You are trying to sell an idea: the idea that people who listen to the radio will want to hear the songs you are promoting.

Bernardo, Promotion Person

As a promotion person for Fibi-Bibi Records, it is my job to make appointments with radio stations. I bring them the company's latest singles (potential hit songs).

I give everything to the music directors and program directors. These are the people who decide what music will be played at the station. The disc jockeys are also important, since they play the records. I try to be as friendly with the people from the radio stations as I can be—sometimes I even take them to dinner!

This job does not require a college degree. It does require an assertive, sales-oriented personality and an ability to work well with others. Salary may start at around $18,000 and could increase to $50,000 or more.

Promotions in Promotion

As a promotion person, you have the opportunity to advance to *promotion manager.* This position places you in charge of everybody who works in the promotion department. Your goal is still the same.

But your responsibilities increase when you become a manager. You must figure out a strategy for promoting the records. This includes knowing what radio stations in which areas attract the right audiences for the music you are promoting. Also, you need to figure out what type of promotion to use for each radio station, from posters and T-shirts to autograph signings.

Salaries for promotion managers range from $21,000 to $90,000 and up.

Publicity

The job of the press agent, or *publicist,* is to get the artist's name into the news.

To be a press agent, it is important to be able to write well. A big part of the job is writing press releases. These are short, one- or two-page news stories about something the artist is doing, like going on tour. Press releases are sent to magazines, television stations, radio stations, and other media.

Small musical groups may consider using a publicist to help advertise their performances.

A press agent also sets up interviews and appearances for the artist. They work almost around the clock. They spend most of their free time *networking*. They do this by going out to parties and nightclubs, trying to meet the right people to help publicize their acts. If you want to be a publicist, you should have a very persuasive personality.

Starting out, you may earn around $15,000 a year, but you could eventually work your way up to a triple-digit salary. It all depends on how hard you work and what contacts you make. Despite the fact that only a high school diploma is really necessary, a college degree in business or journalism can be a big plus.

Buy a beginner's book on writing for public relations and try writing your own press release. Record companies who consider hiring you, even for an internship, will want to see writing samples. If you have a high school newspaper or yearbook, get involved now. The experience will always be valuable.

Taking It on the Road

If you are healthy and energetic, write well, and wouldn't mind attending parties as part of your job, *tour publicist* might be the right position for you. You need to have experience in publicity at any type of company to be considered for this job.

Paulina, Publicist

I started out as a press agent for a small record label. I really liked the job, but when I saw an opening in the newspaper for the position of tour publicist at another record company, I decided to give it a try. I got the job, and now I like it even more than what I was doing before.

As a tour publicist, I do pretty much the same things I used to do, except now I get to travel all over the place. My job is to go on tour with the artist I am promoting and to make sure the public knows about the tour. As we go from city to city, I write press releases, arrange interviews with local radio and TV stations, and make sure journalists and photographers have backstage passes. It's a hectic, crazy job, but it's perfect for me.

Once you become part of a record company's publicity staff, let your boss know you are willing to travel and would enjoy going on tour. Salaries for tour publicists range from $17,000 to $80,000 or more.

More Traveling Opportunities

Another person who needs to accompany an act on tour is the *advance agent.* This person arrives at the next city on the tour long before the artist does, in order to prepare for his or her arrival. They give out backstage passes, hang posters, and deliver any other promotional materials (news stories, photos, tapes, and CDs) to the right radio and TV stations, newspapers, or fan clubs.

No education is required for this position. The only way to find a job of this sort is by word of mouth.

The Concert Hall

A concert hall is like a theater where many different acts come to perform, usually when they go on tour.

As a *concert hall manager,* you would hire and organize people to sell tickets, arrange seating, clean up after a show, keep the performers and audience members safe, and make sure the artists sound and look their best. You may also advertise the shows and find artists to perform at your hall.

A concert hall manager should have very strong business skills. He or she has to do a lot of things using a small amount of money. Many unanticipated problems can come up when organizing a concert, so be prepared to stay calm in a crisis. This job can be highly stressful.

A high-school diploma is the only formal education you need, but you will probably have to start out as a *manager's assistant* in a small concert hall. Over time you will work your way up to the position of manager. At that point you will be able to move on to larger concert halls. Pay starts between $16,000 and $30,000 for smaller halls. Managers of large theaters can make up to $55,000 or more.

The Stage

One of the people that the concert hall manager may hire (or fire) is the *stage manager*. This job is different for each concert hall. The main duties usually include supervising others who control the stage lighting, sound, curtains, backstage area, and dressing rooms.

Trent, Stage Manager

I'm a stage manager, and I'd love to tell you about my job, but I'm very busy right now. Dolly Parton is going to be here in five minutes, and . . . what? She's here now? Okay, Tony, go get some roses for the dressing room, orange juice, and bottled water, too.

I have to go meet with her lighting technician to see if he needs anything. Then I'm organizing a meeting between her sound people and ours. I have to find out when the curtains should open and close and go over my instructions to the security people backstage. Sorry I couldn't talk with you . . . .

Stage managers earn from $12,000 to $40,000 or more, depending on the size and popularity of the hall. It is helpful to understand all kinds of technology. No formal education is necessary. Call local theaters and halls to find out if they are hiring an *assistant stage manager* or gofer.

Promoting Concerts

As a *concert promoter*, you could plan many types of events. This includes small local shows and major music festivals. The promoter is responsible for organizing the event from start to finish. This involves a lot of hard work, patience, and an ability to deal with stress.

A *promoter* needs to supply the money for the show. You can get the money from other people who believe in you. They cover some of the cost. If the show is a success, they gain some of the profits.

You rent the hall for each of the shows you promote. Your duties also include advertising and supervising anybody who works at the show (lighting, sound, security, etc.)

Promoters often put up their own money. Their earnings can range from nothing to millions. Sometimes they even lose money. There is no education required, but it is not a job for people without experience in the music industry. Most concert promoters spend a lot of time in some other position first, such as stage manager or A&R person.

Getting the Gig

As a *booking agent,* your job is to get jobs for musicians. This is done mainly through the mail and over the phone.

Allison, Booking Agent

I think my greatest skill is salesmanship. I can sell anybody anything, so I decided to help some friends in a local band to get gigs, or jobs performing music. I sent photos, tapes, stickers, and other information to some local bars and nightclubs. Then I called each of them to make sure they received everything and tried to talk them into letting the band play there. I also got some of them to agree on a payment for the band's performance.

Booking agents are paid a percentage of what the performers earn. That is why it is a good idea to have a contract signed by the club owner stating how much the musicians will be paid.

Booking agents receive 10 to 20 percent of the performers' earnings, plus expenses. Yearly income can range from $12,000 to as high as $800,000 and up. It all depends on how many engagements you secure.

The best way to get started is to do what

Working in a music store is just one way to be involved in the music industry.

Allison did. Once you gain experience with local acts, you can start sending résumés to booking agencies. Most are located in large cities.

Shop Talk

If you enjoy selling and want to be involved with music, you may want to work in a *music shop*. These types of stores carry all kinds of instruments and equipment, as well as books and sheet music. The best way to get involved with a music store in your area is as a *clerk*.

There are many different duties you could

perform in this position. But helping customers is always part of the job. You need to have a good understanding of all of the items for sale in the store. Customers ask how equipment works, or how difficult an instrument is to learn, or which brand is most appropriate for them. It is the clerk's responsibility to know the answers.

Your salary could range from $12,000 to $25,000 or higher, especially if you earn commission on the items you sell. You need a high school diploma.

Just for the Record

As a *record store salesperson,* your main responsibility would be selling CDs and tapes in a *record store.* You would help customers find certain artists and songs and operate the cash register. Your salary would probably start around minimum wage and increase the longer you worked at that store.

Minding the Shop

Whether you work in a music shop or record store, you always have the potential to become a *manager.* This involves more responsibilities and an increase in salary. If you prove that you are a hard worker and a fast learner, it probably will not matter how much education you have had.

Being a manager means you may decide who works when, and what they must do. You have to deal with any problems that come up, such as angry customers or lazy clerks. You also decide what needs to be ordered for the store.

Salaries for managers range from about $20,000 to as high as $50,000. There are many opportunities in this field for responsible people who work well with others.

Questions to Ask Yourself

Another aspect of the music industry is selling music. 1) Are you a good salesperson? 2) Which job described in this chapter sounds most appealing to you? Why? 3) When the record is produced, would you like to promote it to radio stations?

Other Opportunities

4

Here is a quick rundown on some of the many other opportunities that exist in music.

Jerry, Personal Manager

As the personal manager of a band, my job is to see to it that the band makes it big. I advise them on any types of decisions they are making, whether they are business choices or musical directions.

I have a pretty wide knowledge of the music business. I use that knowledge to create a plan of action for the acts I represent. My earnings completely depend on how much money is made by the artists I work for.

To become a *personal manager*, try managing a small, local act to start out. Or look for job openings with management agencies.

There is a market for every kind of music, from ethnic to pop to rock.

Cecily, Business Manager

I am a business manager rather than a personal manager. I advise the band I manage, but only on their business decisions. I plan their budgets, pay the bills, and try to help the band make as much money as possible.

Business managers earn anywhere from $20,000 to $750,000 yearly, depending on the artists' earnings. The average commission rate is 3 percent to 10 percent. Experience in accounting is helpful.

Jasmine, Music Publisher

I am a music publisher. I buy and sell songs. I listen to demo tapes and go out to bars to hear performers' songs. If I hear something that I think could be a hit, I make them an offer to buy the song.

This is a difficult field to enter without experience. Start out in any position in a record company to gain knowledge of the industry. No college is necessary, and earnings are unlimited.

Floyd, Orchestra Manager

I manage an orchestra. I have to handle any problems that come up, especially when the

An orchestra manager makes sure that everything runs smoothly before, during, and after the orchestra performs.

orchestra is traveling from city to city performing. I help to plan the tour, and I travel with the orchestra.

Salaries for *orchestra managers* range from $15,000 to $60,000 per year. Openings are listed in music-oriented newspapers and newsletters.

Tory, Orchestra Director of Development

My job is to keep the orchestra going financially by raising as many donations from the public as possible. I organize fundraising parties, telethons, mailings, and any other events I can think of.

You may be able to get started as an assistant in this type of position by writing or calling orchestras in your area. Pay for *orchestra director of development* may start as low as $15,000 and could rise to $65,000 or more.

Lila, Orchestra Public Relations Director

It is my job to make sure the public knows about what the orchestra is doing. These things could include concerts, special shows, or fundraising events. I advertise mainly by sending press releases to the media.

The job of *orchestra public relations director* does not require a college degree. Writing skills are important. Send a letter with writing samples to local orchestras, and look for public relations internships.

Johnny, Disc Jockey

I love being a disc jockey. It's fun to play music and talk to people all over the city. I can make jokes and give information on the music that we play. Sometimes I read news and weather reports. It's sort of like being a local celebrity.

Disc jockeys may start out making around $12,000 per year. More successful ones can earn $225,000 or more. It is helpful to have a demonstration tape as a sample of your speaking voice and personality.

Nomi, Music Director

After working as a disc jockey for a few years, I decided to become a music director. That means I pick out music for the disc jockeys to play. I have to have a good idea of who our audiences are, when they are listening, and what they want to hear.

Music directors make between $17,000 and $100,000, depending on the size of the station they work for. Disc jockey experience is required.

Crystal, Program Director

I went from disc jockey to music director. Now I've been promoted to program direc-tor. I decide what type of radio station we should be or become (for example, Top 40 or country?), so that we can gain as many listeners as possible. I also hire and fire disc jockeys.

The starting salary for *program director* may be $17,000 and increase to $100,000 or more. Disc jockey experience is necessary.

Mariel, Video Jockey

I always wanted to be a video jockey, or VJ. Right now I work on a music video show for a local public access channel. I introduce the music videos and report the music news. I hope to work my way up to the top-rated video music networks someday.

If you are very lucky, a career as a *video jockey* can lead to a great deal of money and fame. If you work on public access or a college TV station, which are good places to start, you will probably have to work for free. You could earn $300,000 or higher per year at the major networks.

Buddy, Music Teacher

I am a music teacher at a high school. I give lessons to the students and organize the school band. Sometimes we play performances

Teaching a young student how to sing or play an instrument can be a
satisfying and fulfilling career.

for parents, which I plan and stage.

Music teachers for schools make between $20,000 and $60,000. The job requires at least four years of college plus some time in student teaching.

Private teachers earn from $10 to $75 per hour. They should have many years of training in one or more instruments.

Janet, Music Journalist

I review records and concerts in my daily column in a local newspaper. I hope to work for a music magazine some day, reporting on the hottest trends and interviewing music stars.

Most newspapers and magazines are looking for writers with college degrees. Pay for *music journalists* ranges from $15,000 to more than $100,000. Many newspapers offer internships.

Questions to Ask Yourself

Music has still more careers to offer. 1) Would you like to manage a band? 2) Could you buy and sell songs for your company? 3) Would you enjoy managing an orchestra?

The Demonstration Tape

5

Most jobs require a résumé. For many of the careers in the music world, your demonstration tape, or demo, serves as your introduction. If you can afford it, you can also have your demo recorded on a CD. Check the classified section of music magazines.

Once you have recorded a demo, the following are tips on how best to use it.

The Demo and the Job

The demo can help you get a job performing at a nightclub or bar. Call the places where you are interested in performing, and ask when it would be most convenient for you to drop off a demo tape.

When you meet with the owner or manager, they will probably ask you a few questions about your music and image. Make sure you give them your telephone number so they can call you back after listening to the tape. If they

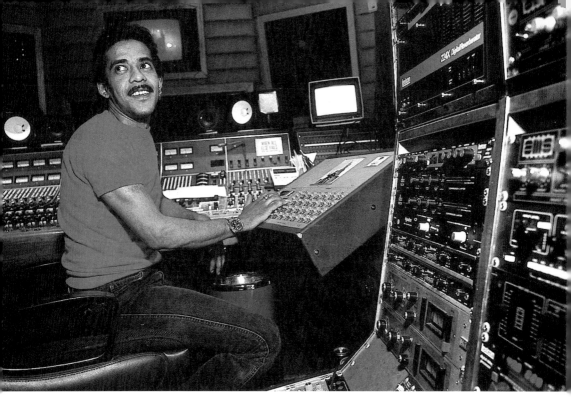

You can record your own demo tape or you can hire a recording engineer to help you.

like it, they may offer you an opportunity to play on a night that is not very popular. It will be an *audition*. You should always take these jobs, even if they do not pay. They often lead to better offers.

If you are a booking agent, the process is the same. But you, rather than the musicians, will arrange everything.

The Demo and the Record Company

Your demo could also serve as your key to open the door to a recording contract. The first step is to find record companies that specialize in the type of music you play. You can get started by checking the list at the back of this book, then continue your search at your public library. You will need to find the addresses of as many companies as possible.

To make your demo look professional, have some labels made at a *tape duplication company*. You can find these companies in the Yellow Pages under "Recording service—sound and video." On the label, include the following: Your name or the name of your band, your address and telephone number, the names of the songs on the tape, and the length of each song (for example, *I'll Open The Door [4:15]*). Include this information on the tape cover too, which can also be professionally made by the tape duplication company.

The tape duplication company can also make copies of your demo for you. However, this is more expensive than making copies of your demo yourself. Call the record company before mailing your demo. Ask the receptionist for the name of the A&R person who listens to the demo tapes. You will be sending your tape to this person's attention.

Hungry Jack Records
ATTN: Jeff Pancake, A&R
2929 Maple Road
Waffle, CA 98989

Along with your demo, you should send: neatly typed lyrics to each of the songs on the tape; a one-page description of your music; your accomplishments as an artist; and any other information you want to use to sell yourself. Try to include some good photos of you or your band, and enclose everything in a two-pocket folder.

If you are a personal manager for a performer or band, the process is the same. But you are the one who will call the record company and send the demo.

Best of luck on your venture into a career in music!

Questions to Ask Yourself

In the music business, your demo is often your résumé. 1) Do you know how to make a demo? 2) Do you know how to package it professionally to send it to the record company?

Glossary

A&R Artist and Repertoire; the part of a record company that seeks new talent.

concert hall Theater where artists perform.

copyright Legal action that protects original songs from being used without permission.

demonstration tape (demo) Tape an aspiring musician, songwriter, disc or video jockey makes to prove his or her talent.

free lance Working for many employers.

independent record company Small record company, not one of the major ones.

internship Unpaid position one takes in order to gain experience in an industry.

multi-track recorder Inexpensive device that can be used to create a demo.

music theory How music works.

networking Getting to know people who may help you in the future.

press release Short news story.

single Potential hit song.

For Further Reading

Davison, Marc. *All Area Access: Personal Management for Unsigned Musicians.* Milwaukee, WI: Hal Leonard Corporation, 1997.

Gerardi, Robert. *Opportunities in Music Careers.* Lincolnwood, IL: VGM Career Horizons, 1997.

Halloran, Mark, ed. *The Musician's Business and Legal Guide.* Englewood Cliffs, NJ: Prentice-Hall, 1996.

Johnson, Jeff. *Careers for Music Lovers and Other Tuneful Types.* Lincolnwood, IL: VGM Career Horizons, 1997.

Levine, Michael. *The Music Address Book: How to Reach Anyone Who's Anyone in Music.* New York: HarperCollins Publishers, Inc., 1994.

McGlothin, Bruce. *Careers Inside the World of Sports and Entertainment.* New York: Rosen Publishing Group, 1995.

For More Information

Music Organizations

American Federation of
   Musicians
1501 Broadway, Suite 600
New York, NY 10036

American Society of Music
   Arrangers and Composers
P.O. Box 17840
Encino, CA 91416

American Society of Music
   Copyists
P.O. Box 2557
Times Square Station
New York, NY 10108

Audio Engineers Society, Inc.
60 East 42nd Street
New York, NY 10165

In Canada:
75 The Donway West, Suite
   1010
Don Mills, Ontario
Canada M3C 2E9

Music Publishers

Alexis
P.O. Box 532
Malibu, CA 98265

DRG Music
130 West 54th Street
New York, NY 10019

Opryland Music Group, Inc.
65 Music Square West
Nashville, TN 37015

Star International, Inc.
P.O. Box 470346
Tulsa, OK 74147

Record Labels

20hz Records
1995 Oak Street #2
San Francisco, CA 94117
Web site: http://www.twenty-
   hz.com
dance music

A & M Records
1416 North LaBrea Avenue
Los Angeles, CA 90028
Web site: http://www.
   amrecords.com
various types of music

AD Music
Attn: Steve Farmer, ADML
   (A&R)
P.O. Box 3021

Littlehampton
West Sussex BN162NX
England
Web site: http://tile.net/
   admusic/
electronic/experimental

Atomic Theory
106 West 49th Street
Minneapolis, MN 55409
www.tt.net/atomic
E-mail: atomic@tt.net
rock

Cexton Records
P.O. Box 80187
Rancho Santa Margarita, CA
   92688
Web site: http://www.cexton.
   com

E-mail: john@cexton.com
jazz

Delmore Recordings
2400 Oakland Avenue
Nashville, TN 37212
www.panix.com/~delmore
E-mail: delmores@aol.com
various types of music

Delos International
Hollywood and Vine Plaza
1645 North Vine Street, Suite
   340
Hollywood, CA 90028
Web site: http://www.delosmus.
   com
feedback@delosmus.com
classical

Internet Sites

www.musiciansnetwork.com
Music information, bulletin boards, sound samples, news

www.music.org/pubs/interdir/listing.html
International directory of music organizations

www.fisica.edu.ny/pages/disco.html
Record labels on the net

www.artstozoo.org/artslynx/music.htm
National music resources online

www.artswire.org/artsites/music.html
Comprehensive listing of orchestras

Index

About the Author

John Giacobello is a musician and free-lance writer who resides in New York City. Before moving to New York, he wrote music and fashion-related articles for various newspapers and magazines in Pittsburgh. He also had training in several instruments, including guitar, piano, flute, and clarinet.

Mr. Giacobello is currently the guitarist, keyboard programmer, backup vocalist, and songwriter for an alternative rock band called Edrazeba.